A LITERARY HISTORY OF ROME IN THE SILVER AGE

From Tiberius to Hadrian

By
J. WIGHT DUFF
Edited by A. M. DUFF

BARNES & NOBLE, INC.
NEW YORK

Second edition 1960

Printed in Great Britain